This coloring book for adults is dedicated to my mother, JoAnn Cameron, who loved flowers, both wild and domestic. She always had beautiful flowers in her yard in Paul, Idaho and would float a rose or peony in a dish on the kitchen table. She also had a gorgeous bed of wildflowers that my dad seeded each spring and tended throughout the summer at "the cabin" in Ketchum.

It is my hope that coloring these images brings you joy.

Tamara A. Cameron

ColorBinge™
Unique Art for Colorists

Welcome to the ColorBinge worldwide family! We would love to see your colored pages! Please join our Private Facebook Group at https://www.facebook.com/groups/ColorBinge/ or just search for ColorBinge on Facebook.

You can find out more about us and all we do on our website at www.ColorBinge.com.

I am also on Instagram as @ColorBinge.

We spend most of our time on Facebook, though, so join us there!

Color the Rural West
Flowers Wild & Domestic

Coloring book design by **Tamara A. Cameron**
Photography by **David R. Day**

Larger full color photographs and an online greyscale coloring guide can be found at **www.colorbinge.com/greyscale**

Please note: *The title of each image is on the back of the image. Our thought was, that if you colored the image and wanted to give it to someone else, the title would travel with your finished artwork.*

Pages at the end of this book have intentionally been left blank so colorists have a place to test their colors on this medium.

First Printing
2016

www.colorbinge.com

Greyscale Coloring Tips

Make a little plan. Decide on your color scheme. Test your pencils, pens or markers on the test pages in the front and back of the book to ensure your colors are the shades you want them to be.

Keep it simple, especially if you are a beginner. You don't have to choose 12 shades of blue. You literally can choose one medium shade and use varying amounts of pressure and get great results.

Expect your greyscale to look messy and like it's not going to work out. Part of the magic of greyscale coloring is that it starts to look amazing during about the last 1/3 of the coloring.

Layer, layer, layer. Start with a light touch and darken areas only when you can see what to darken. I often color a whole area with light layers and then go back to add layers when it's so clear what needs to be done that I just can't stand it any longer. Doing it this way makes the picture come alive! It's a little reward and inspires me to carry on.

Use the greyscale as your guide. The shadows and highlights are already there. All you have to do is follow along. Use light colors in the light grey areas, mid-tones in the medium grey areas and your darkest colors in the dark grey areas.

You don't have to choose realistic colors. Create a bright pink truck or a purple sky! If you do want to go realistic, see how mother nature colors it. Google whatever you are coloring, then choose "Images" at the top of the page, or refer to the full color versions of these pages on the back cover or at www.colorbinge.com/greyscale.

You will need a white pencil or pen. No matter what, there are going to be white areas that you want to stand out more when you are finished. You will love your white pencil or pen.

Don't be afraid to use your grey colored pencil to darken any areas of grey that you feel are going to get "lost" as you add color.

If you are intimidated by a large greyscale, print a downloadable one smaller than full-size. Most printer software will allow you to reduce the size of the page you are printing. Choose file, then choose print, and look for options to reduce size on the print screen.

Practice! Spend some time trying different techniques on different areas of the same picture so you can compare results. When you find your magic formula, write it down. Then pitch your practice sheet in the recycle and move on with confidence!

If you are new to greyscale coloring, give it some time and two or three practice sheets. Be kind to yourself while you color. It's all just a fun learning experience. Before long you will be coloring greyscale images like a pro!

The most important thing to do is Have Fun!

Test Page

Try your pencils, pens and markers here. Every paper is different. This page has been intentionally left blank so you can use it as a test page. There are also blank test pages in the back of the coloring book.

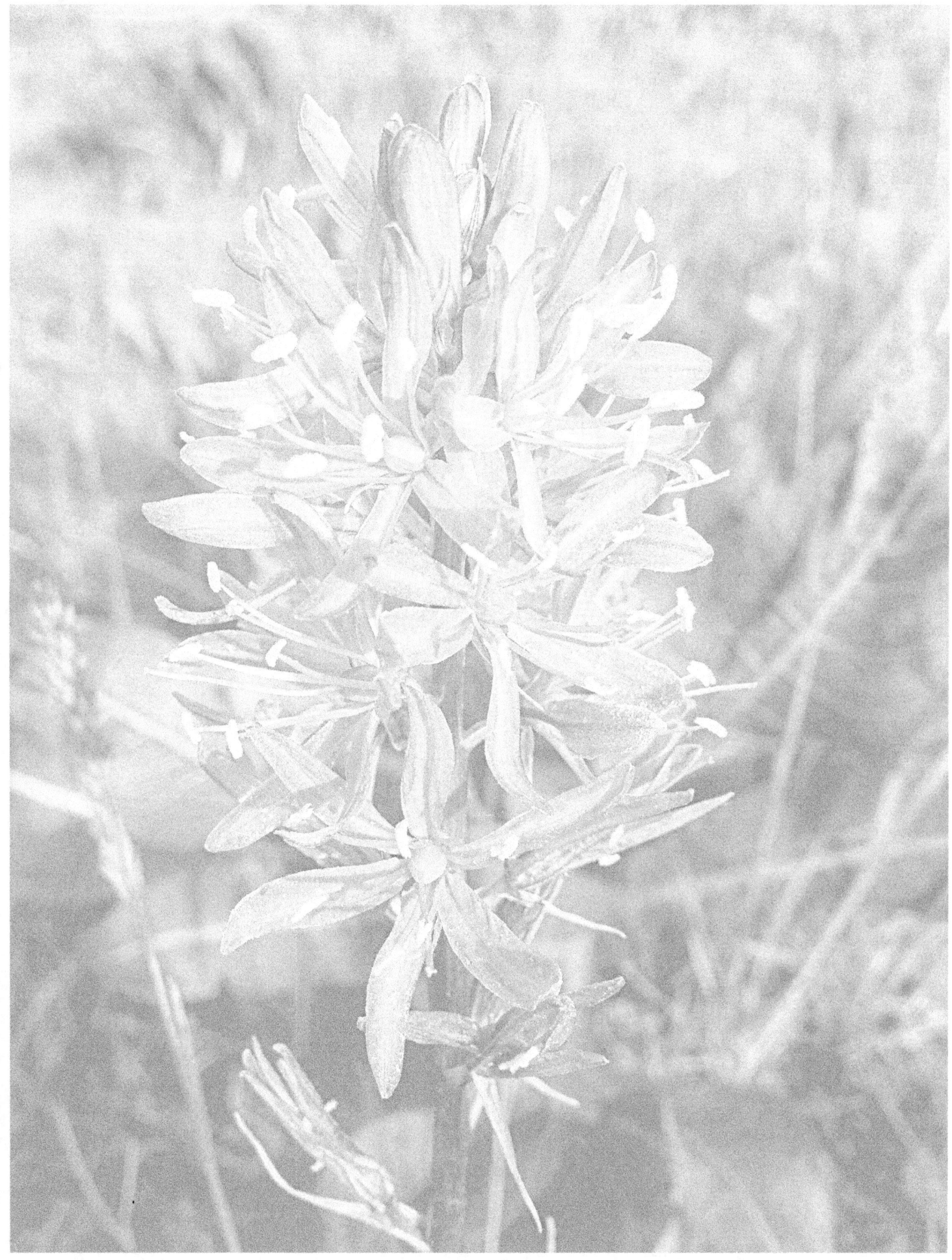

Larkspur

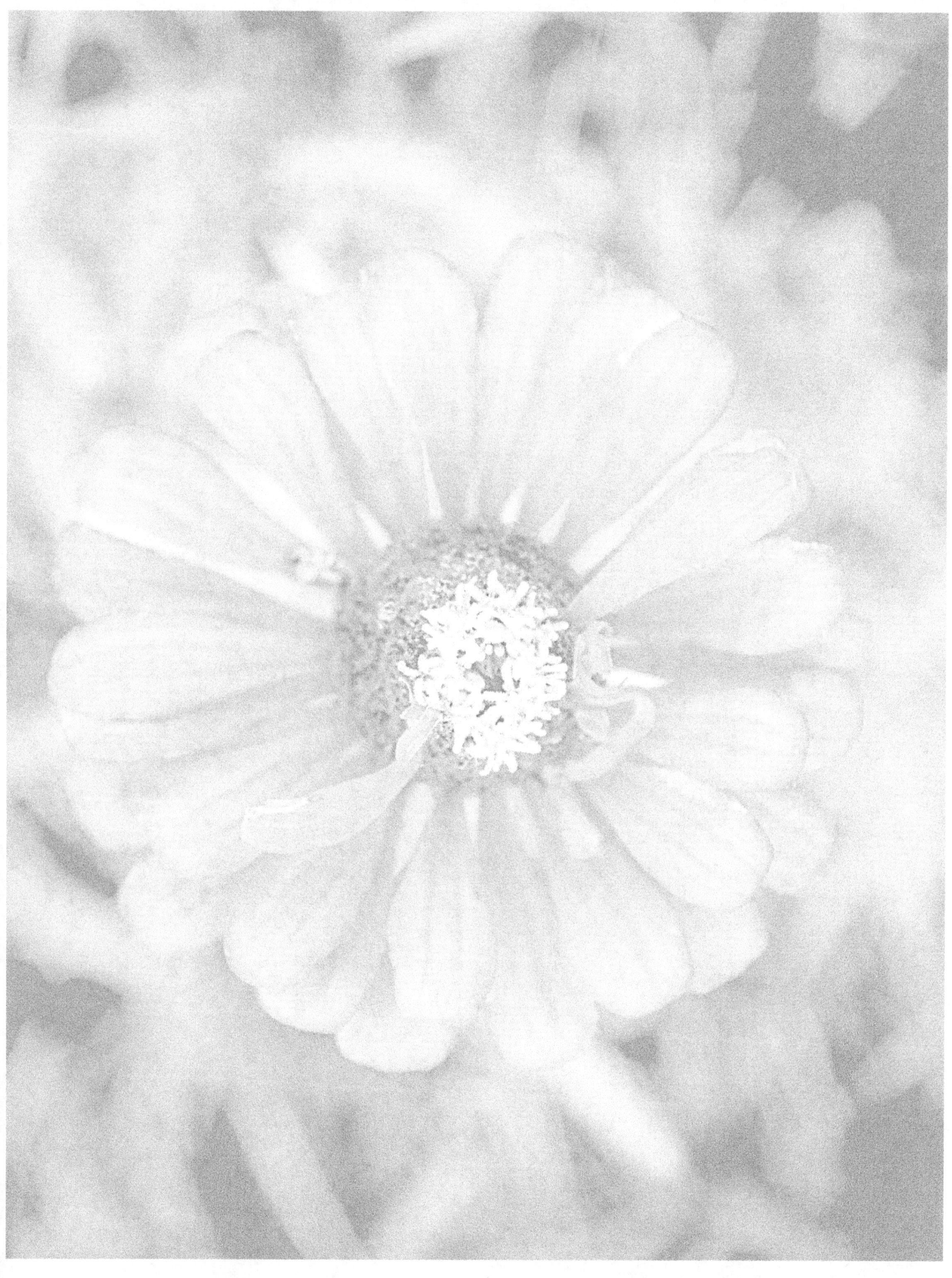

Zinnia

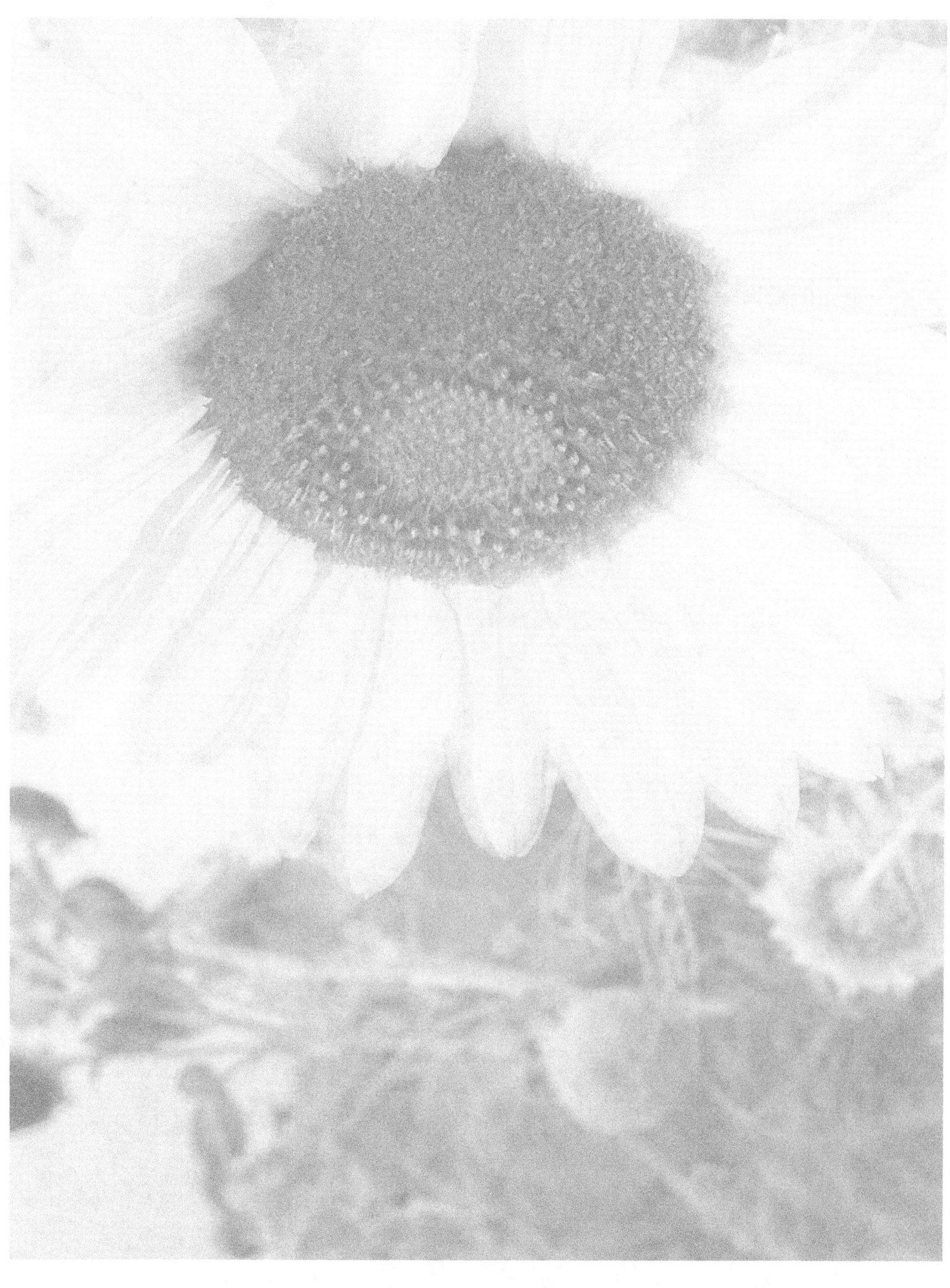

Sunflower

Bed of Zinnias

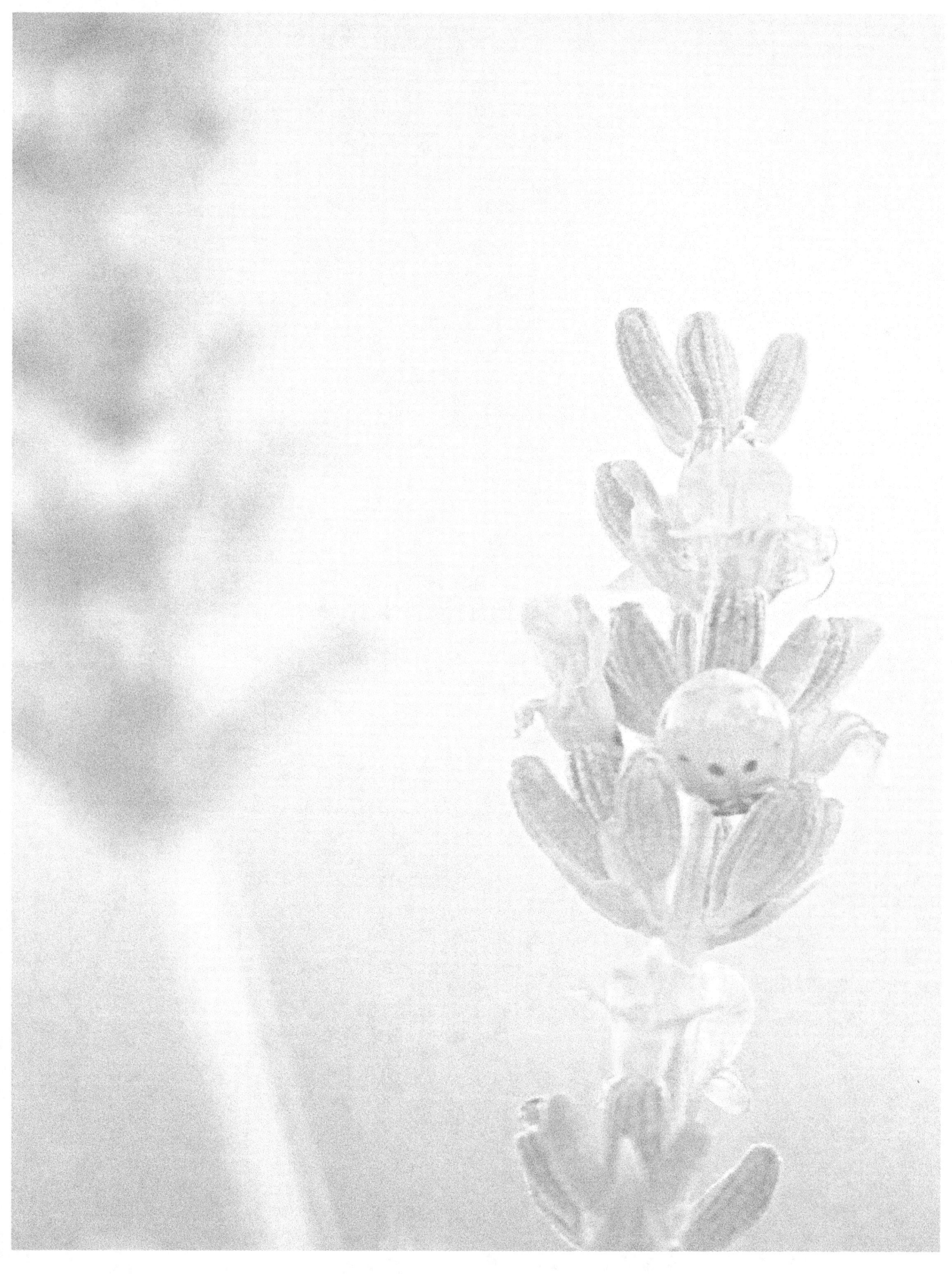

Lavendar With a Friend

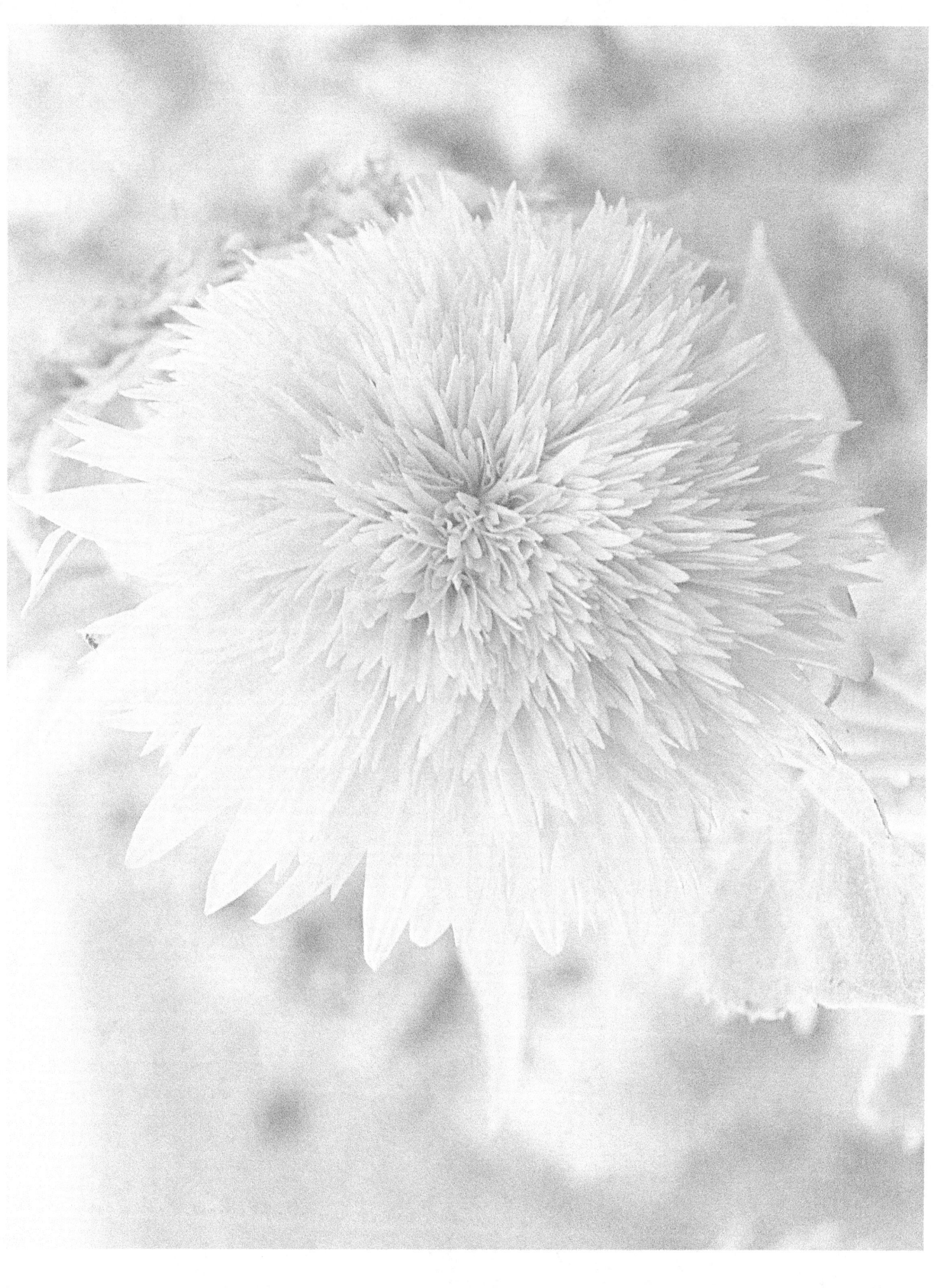

Teddy Bear Sunflower

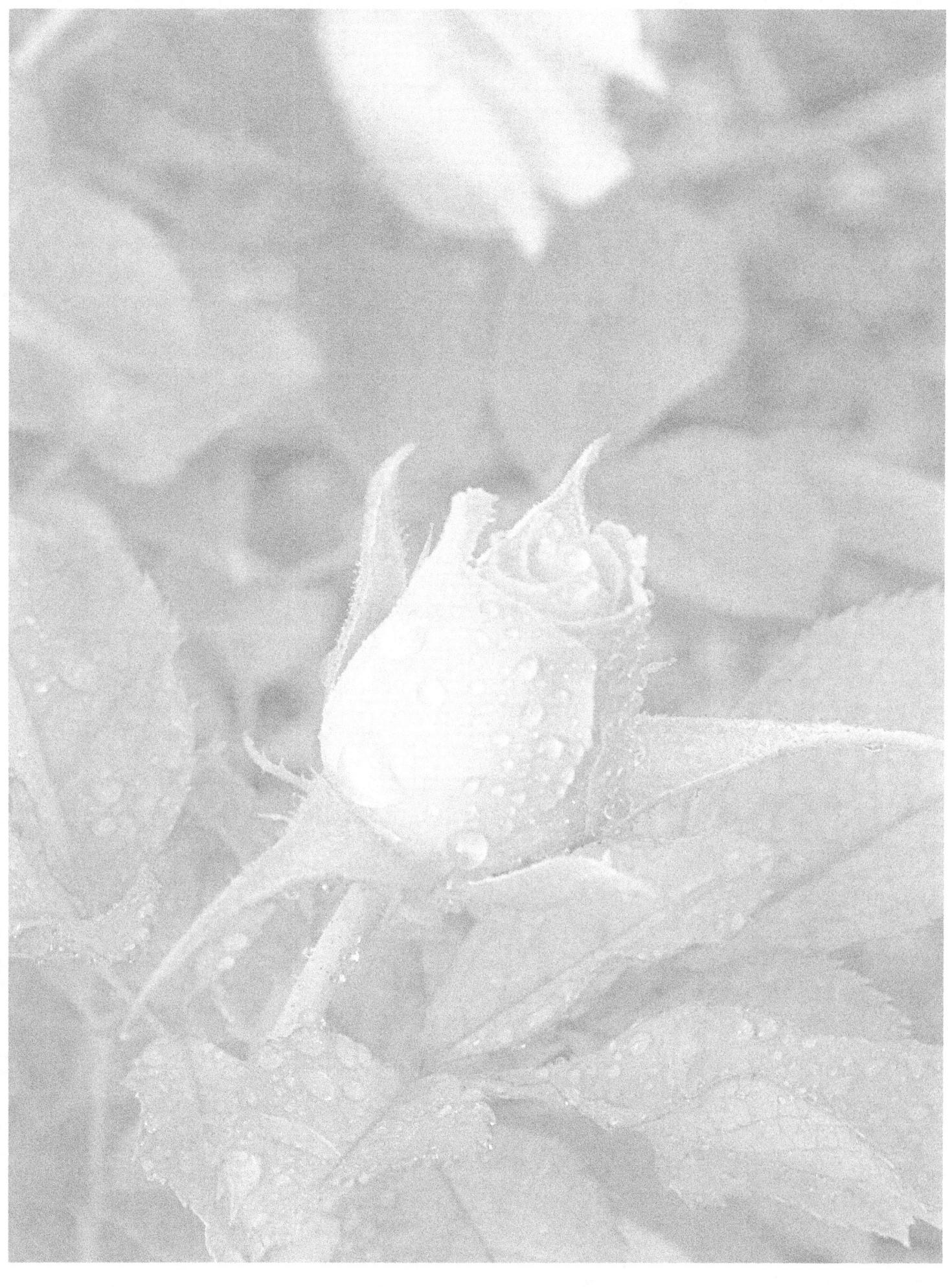

Domestic Rosebud

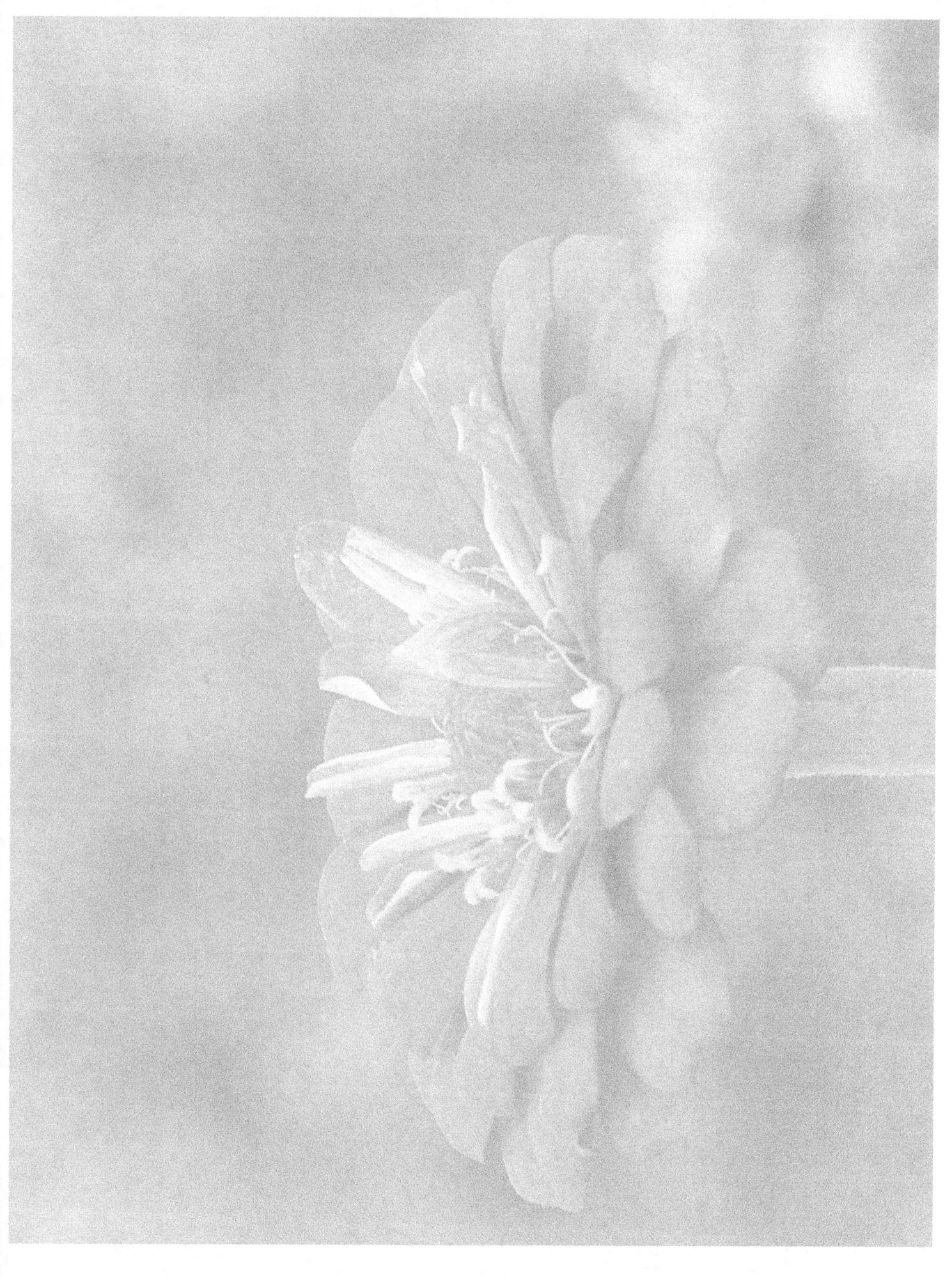

Zinnia

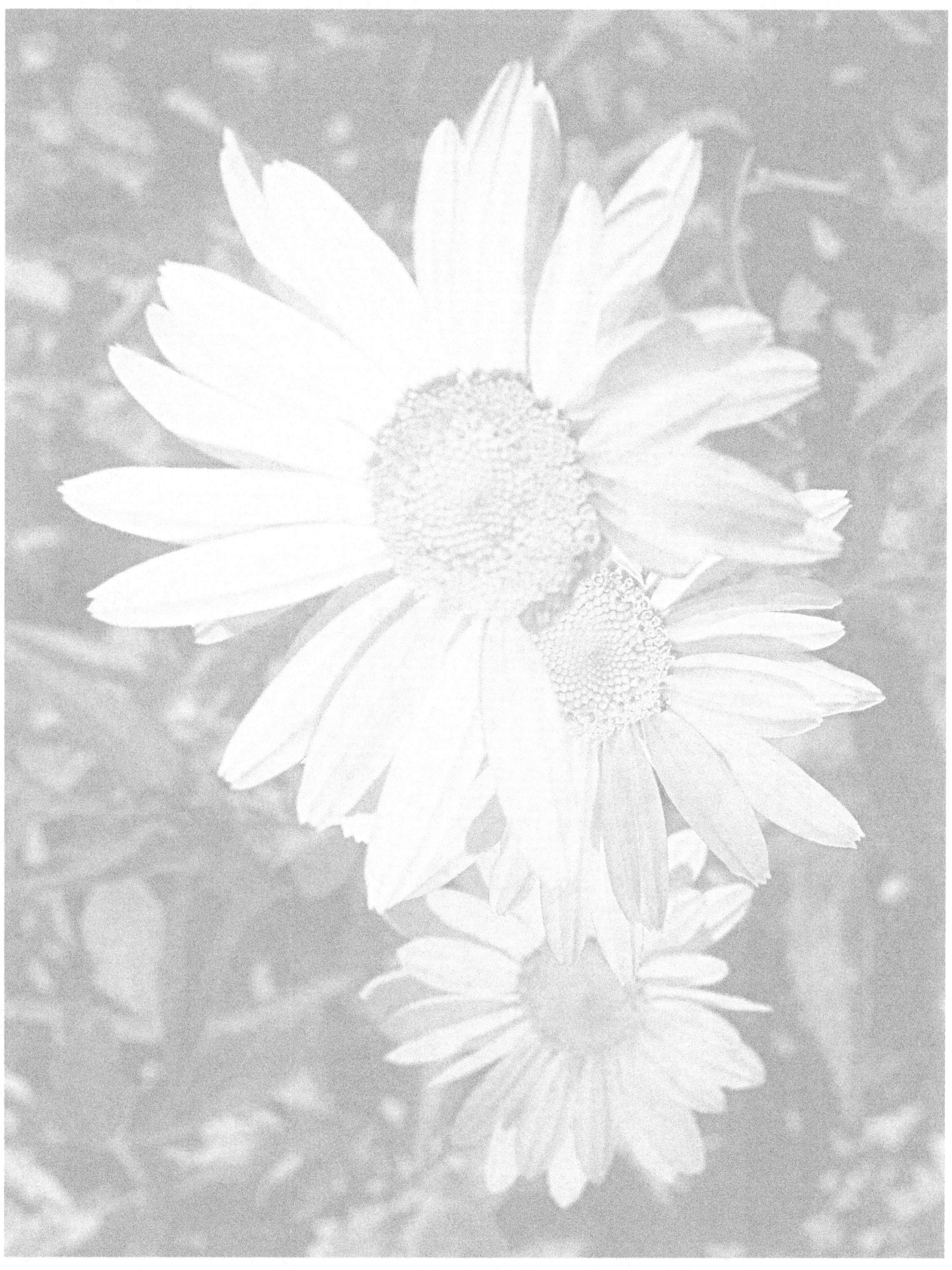

Shasta Daisies

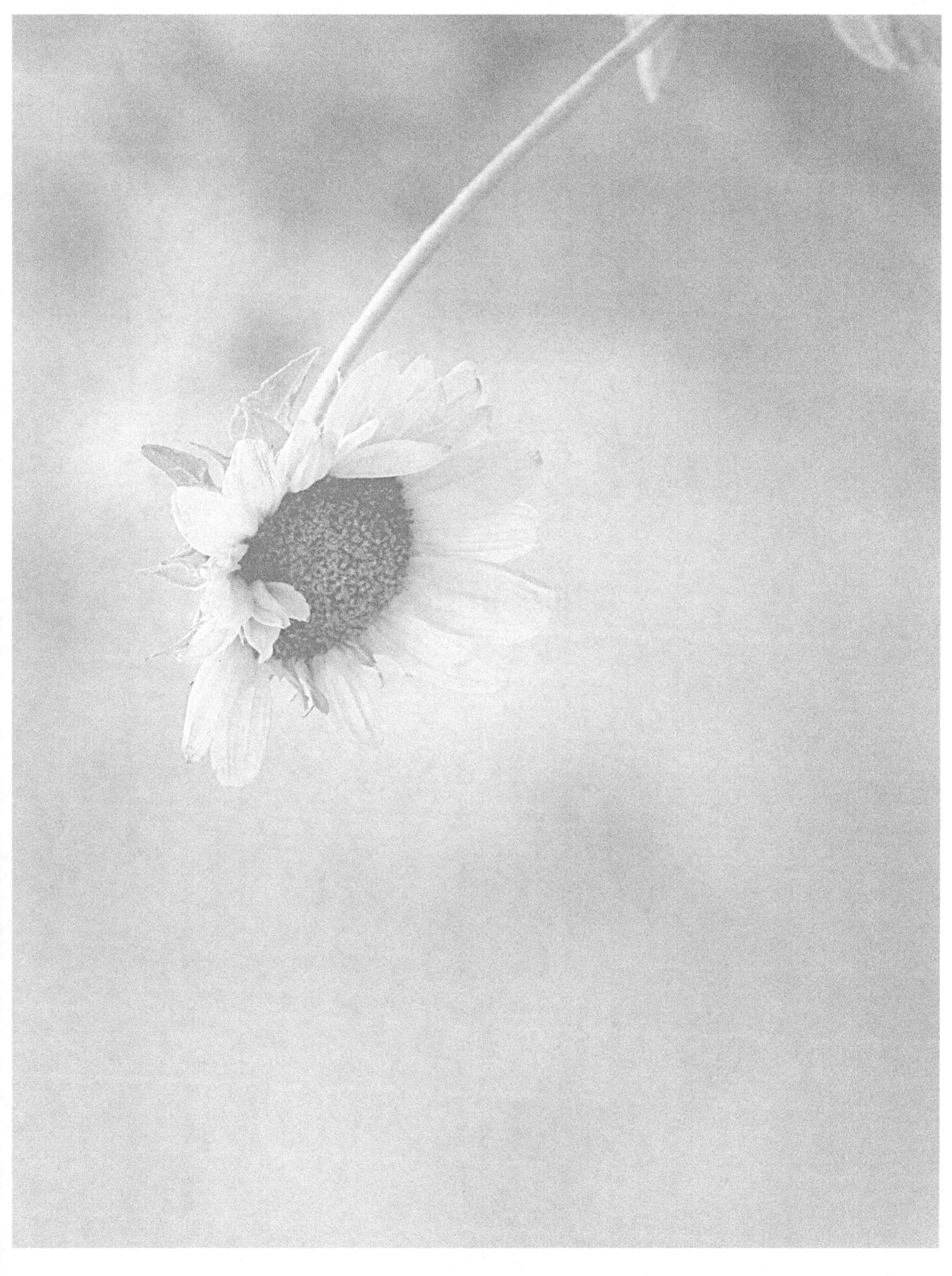

Wild Sunflower

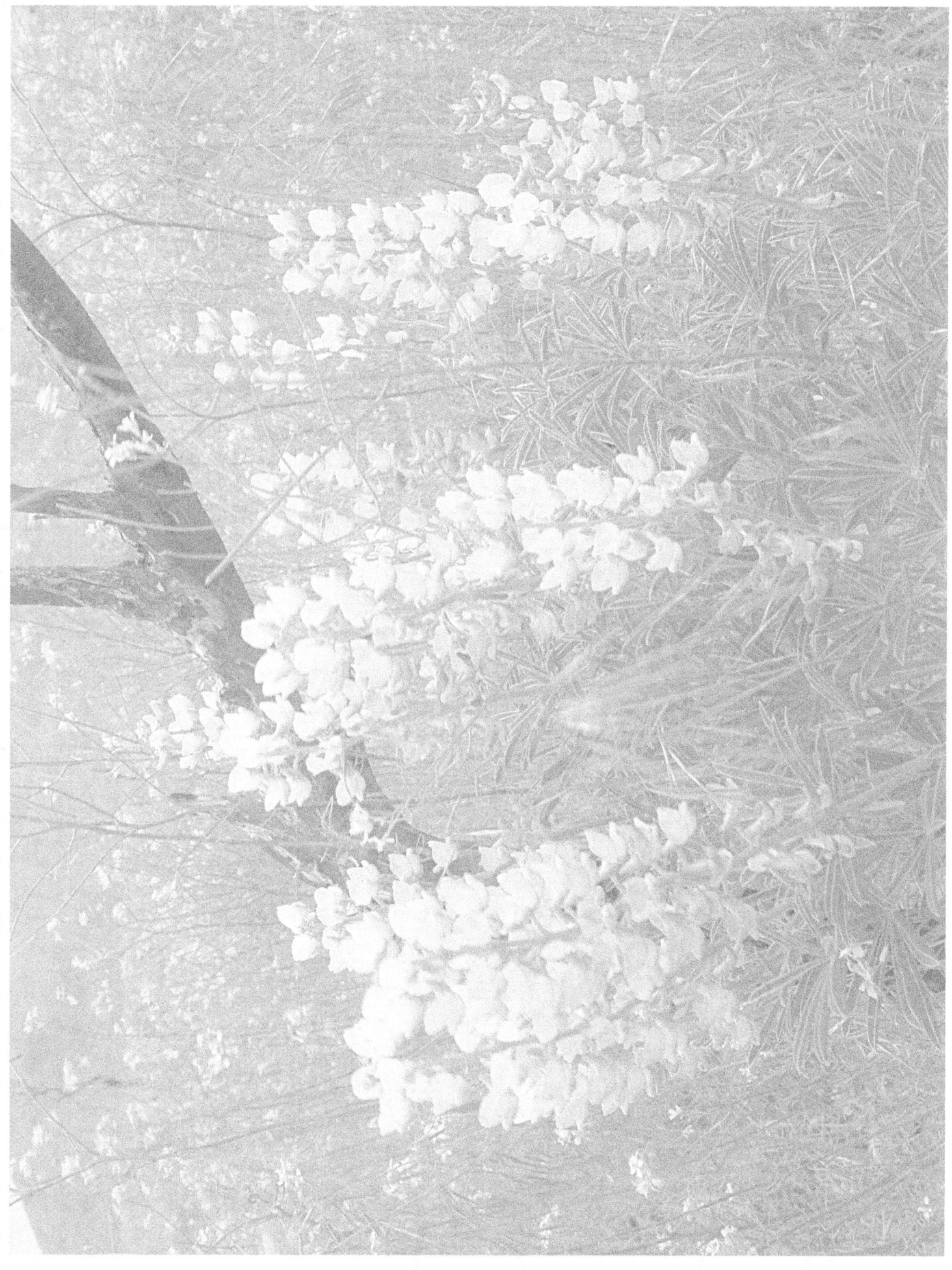

Lupine

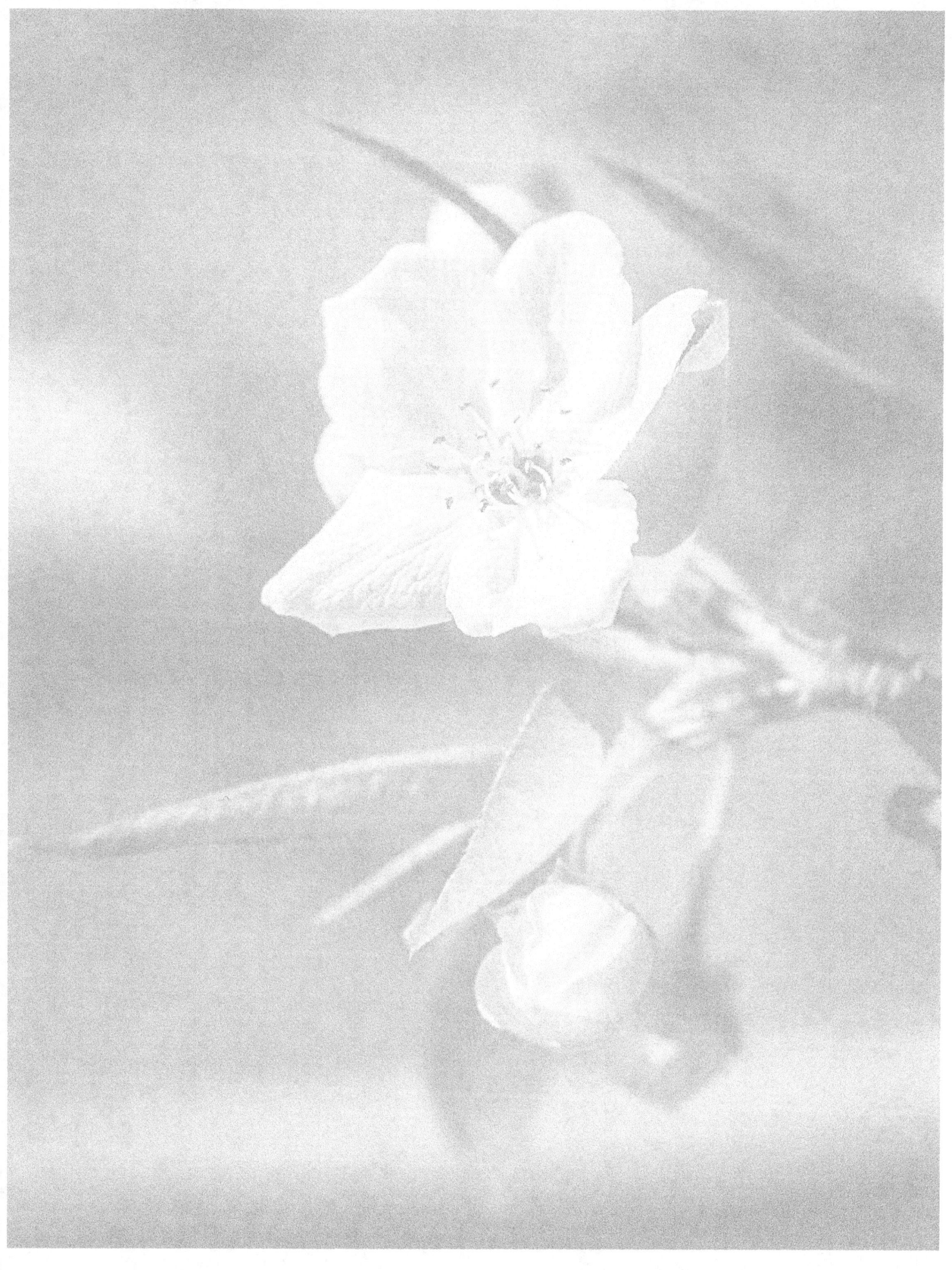

Apple Blossoms

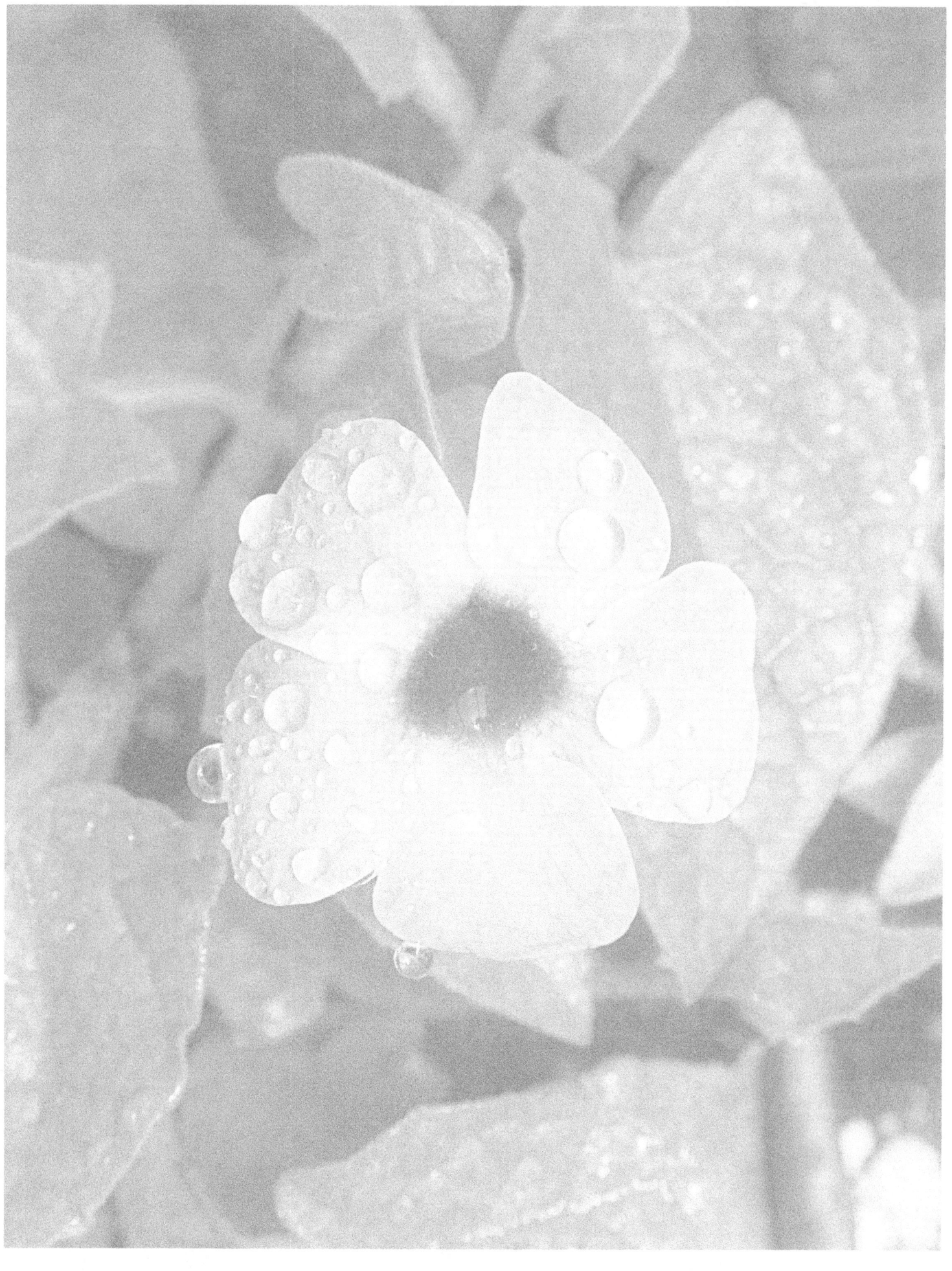

Black Eyed Susan

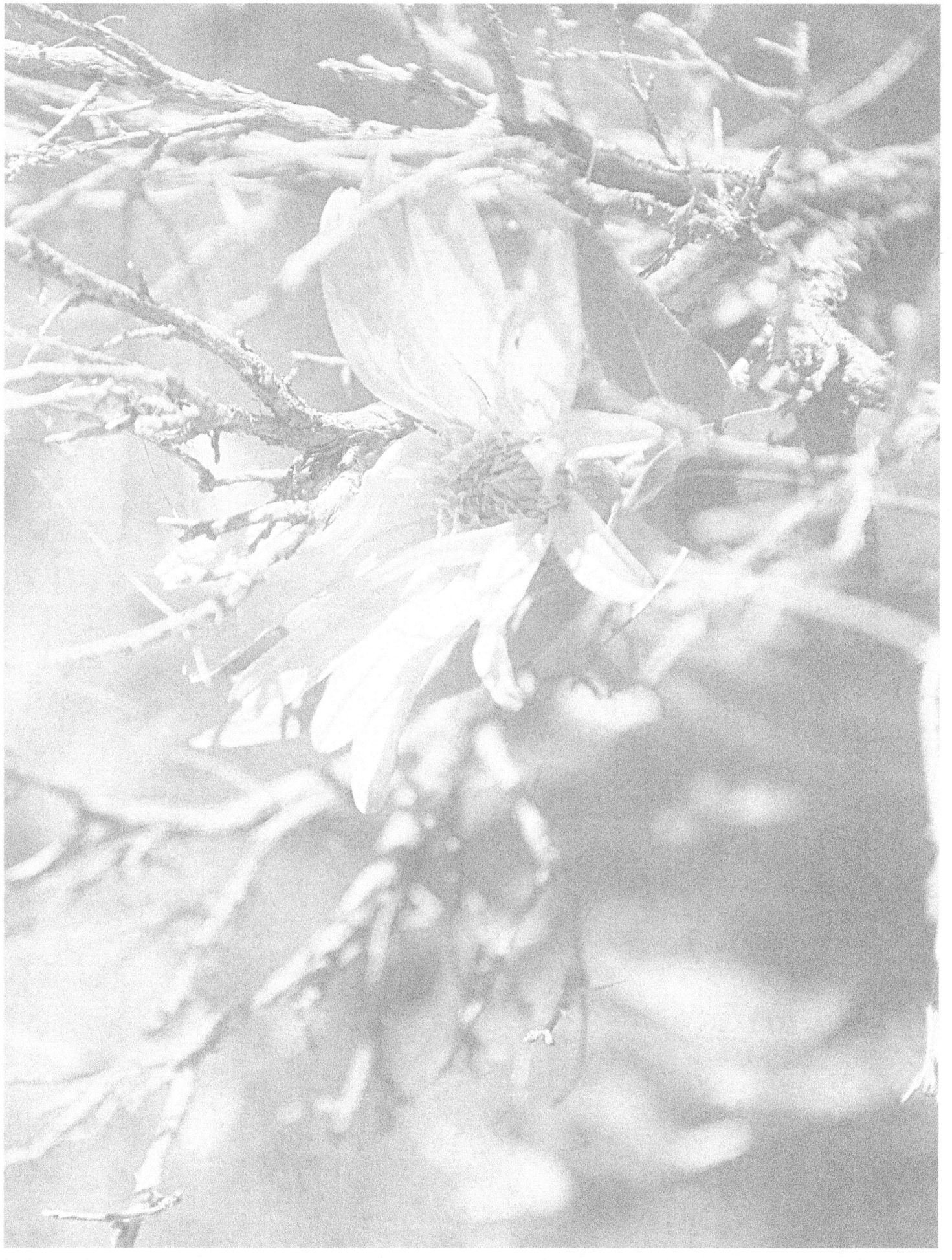

Bush Sunflower

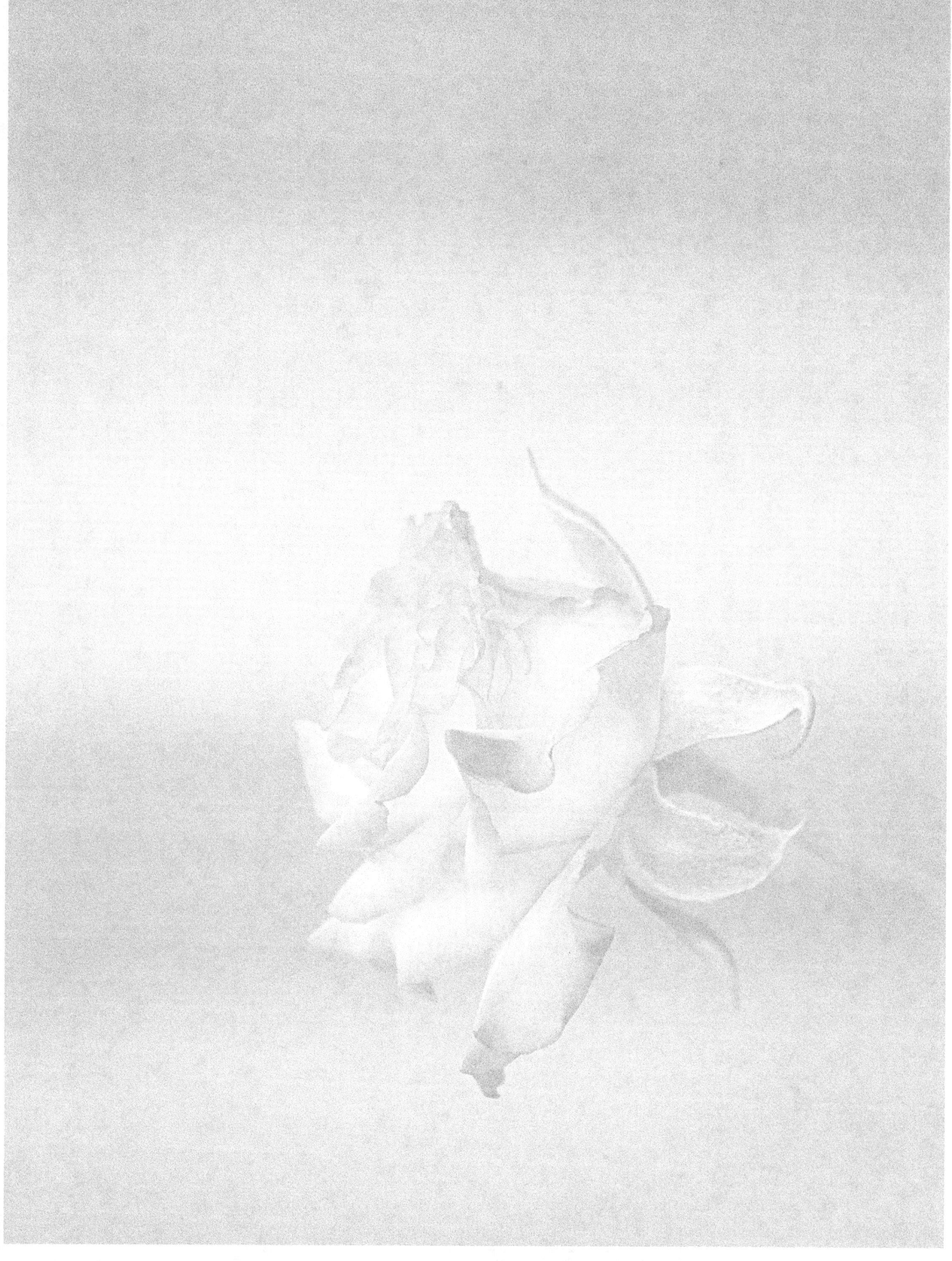

Domestic Rose

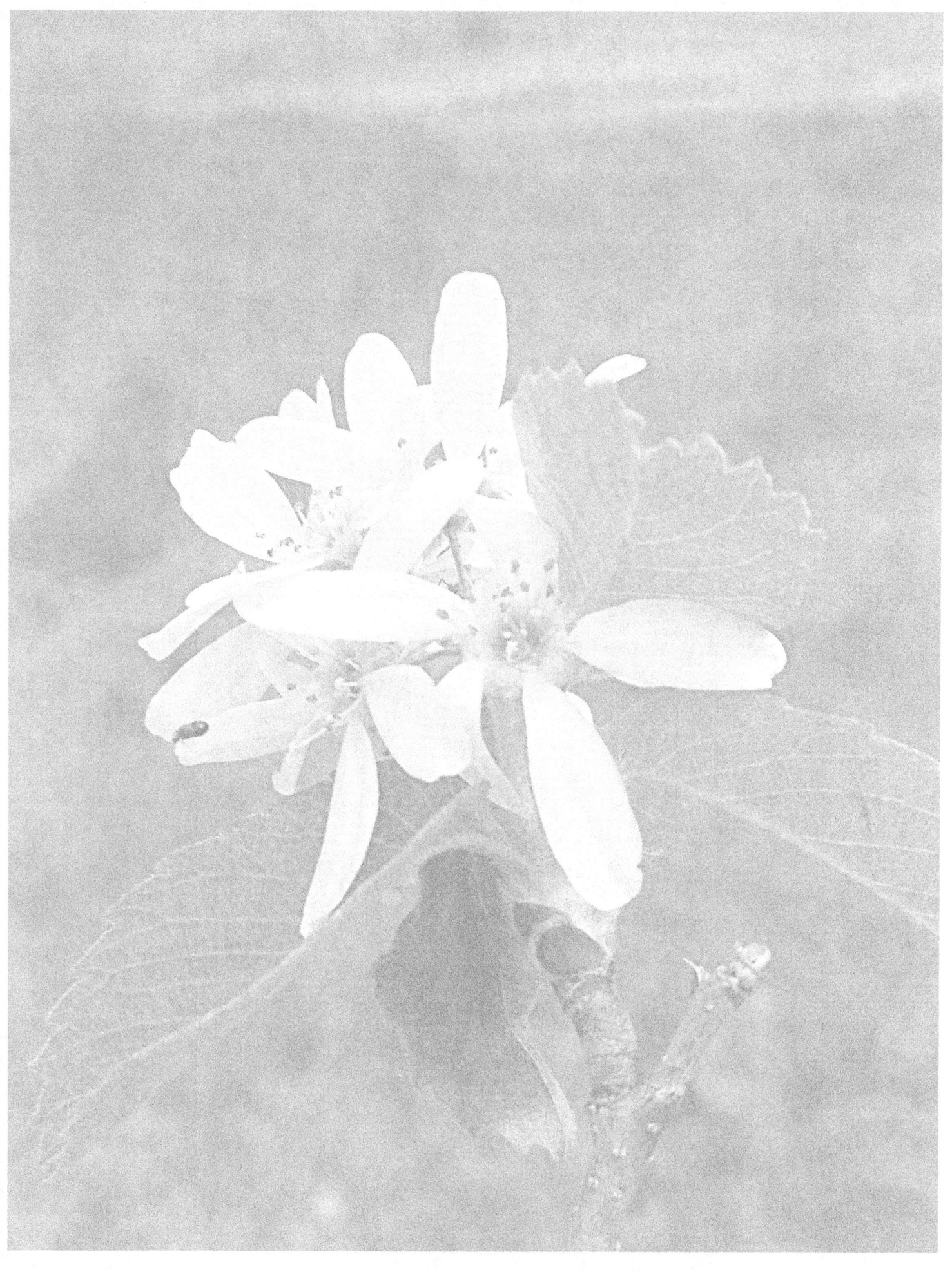

Syringa

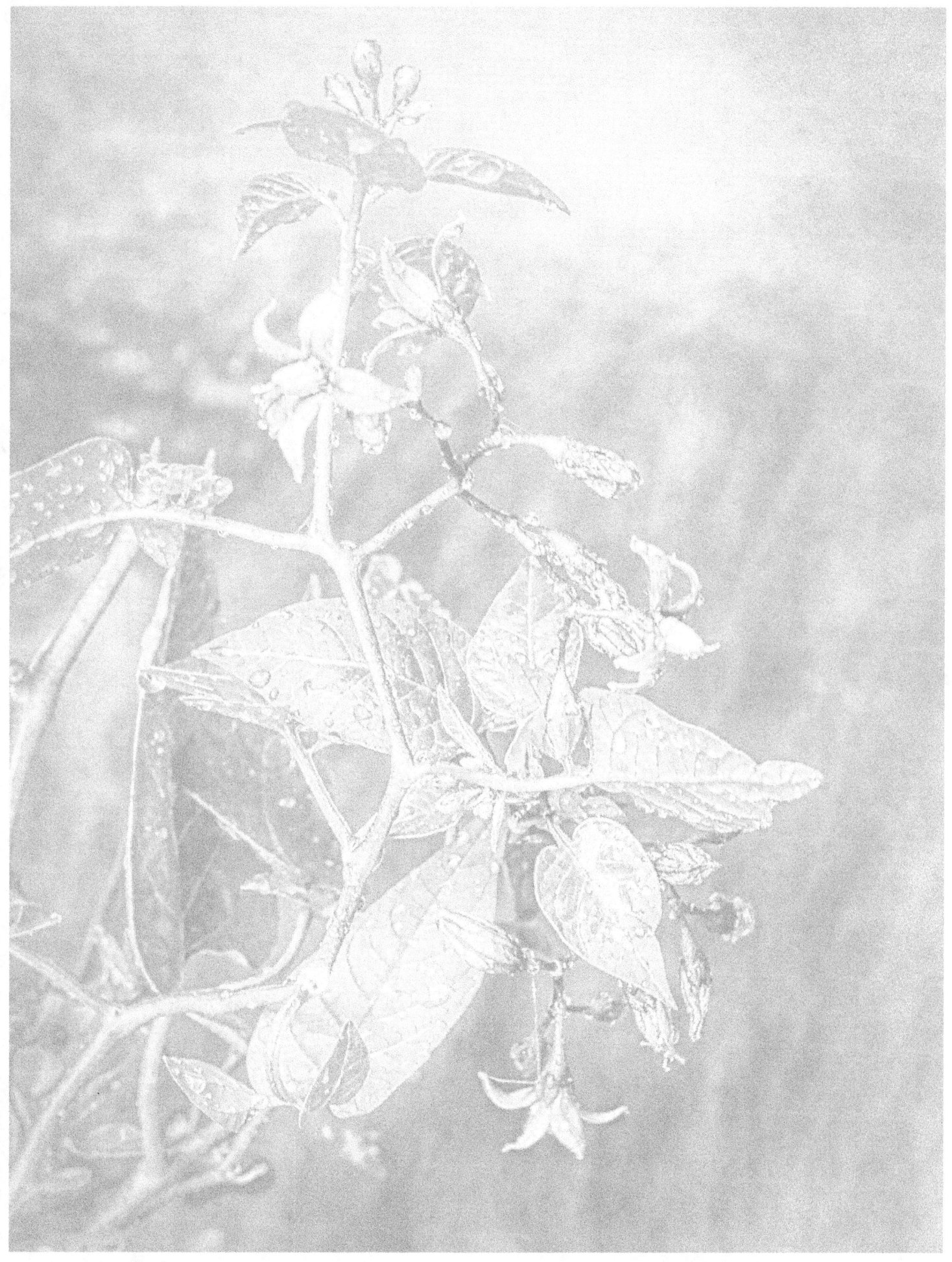

Nightshade

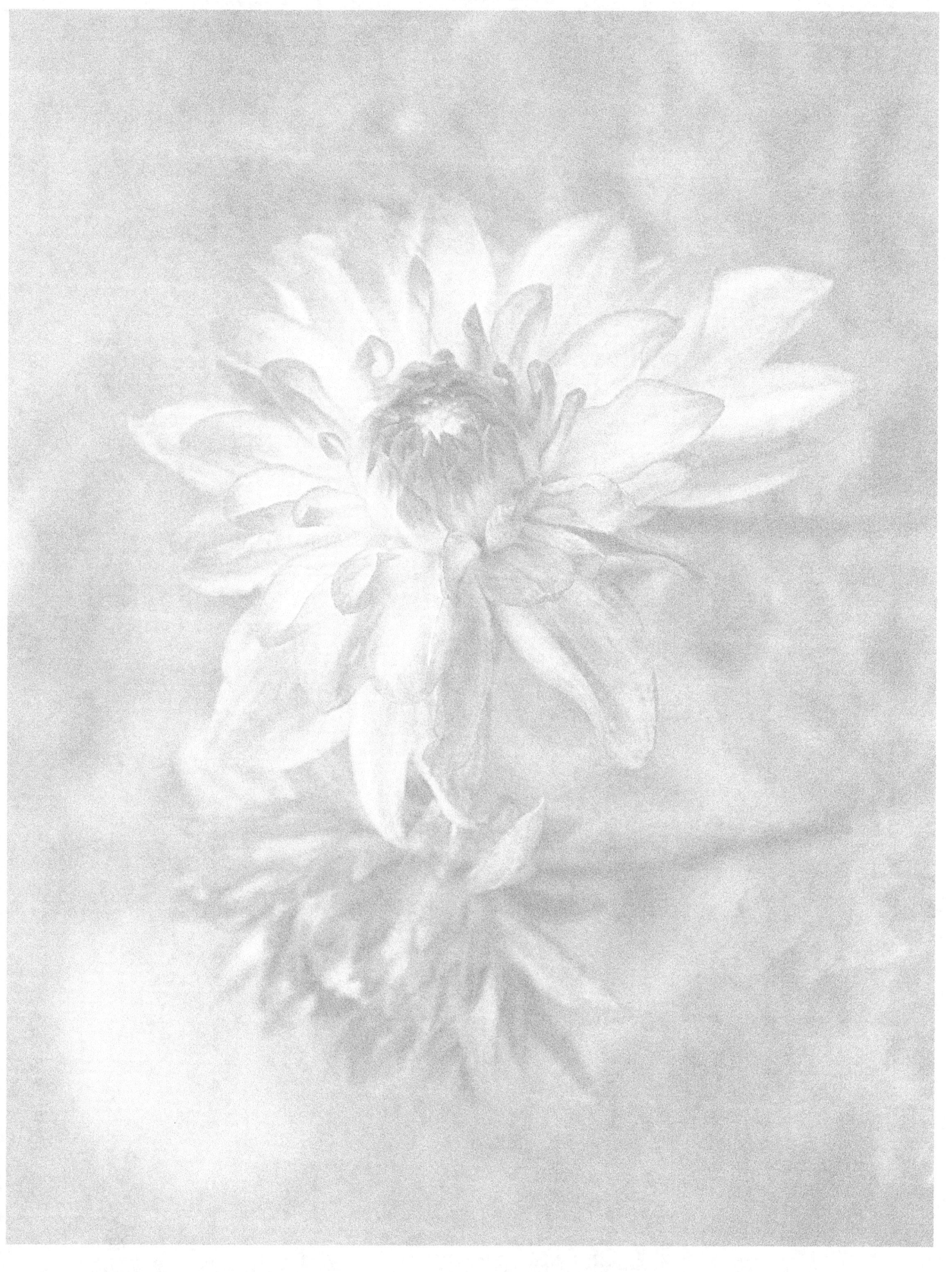

Chrysanthemum

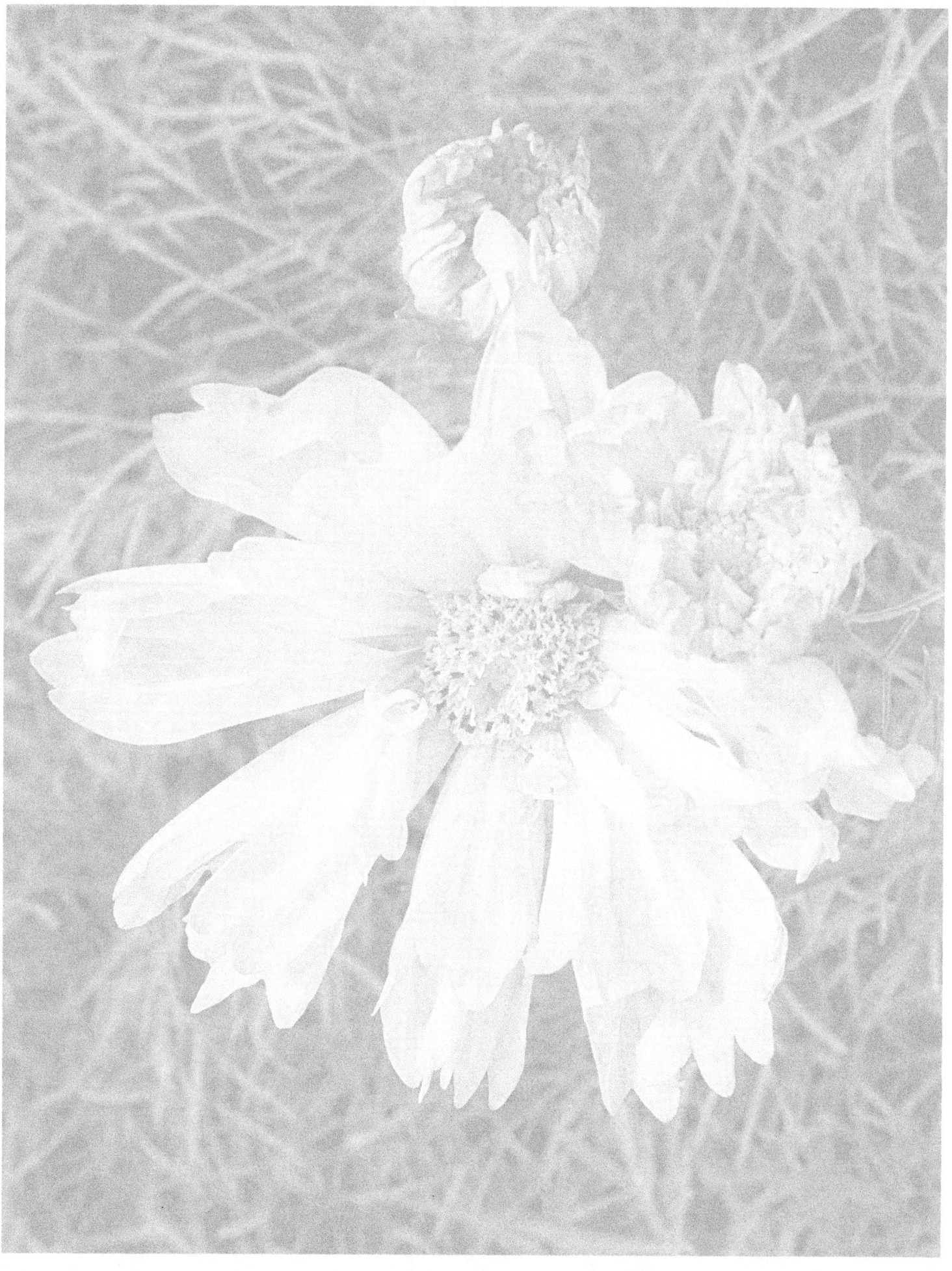

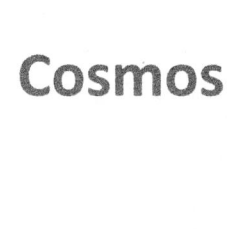

Cosmos

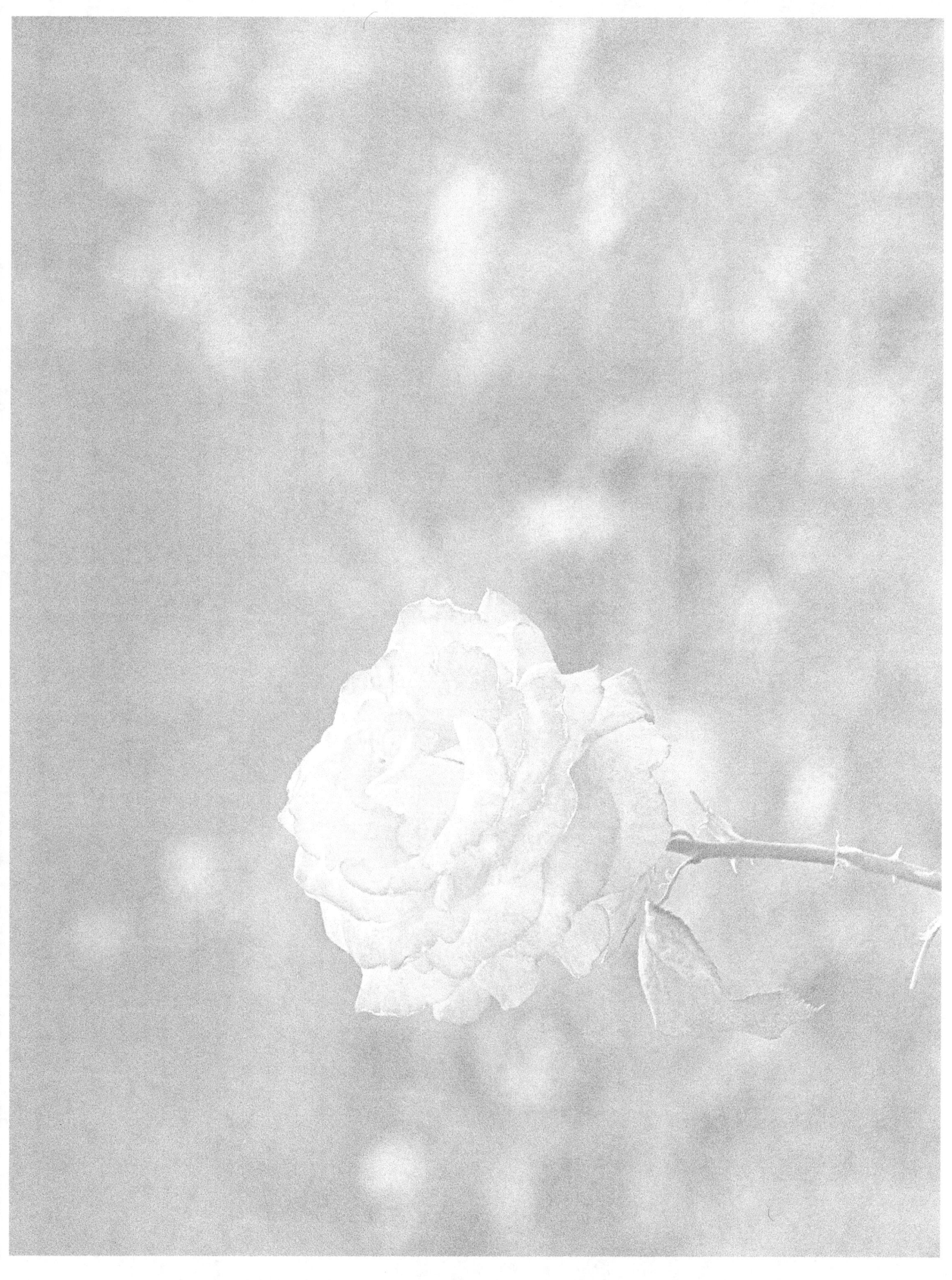

Domestic Rose